Sagittarius

Also by Sally Kirkman

Aries
Taurus
Gemini
Cancer
Leo
Virgo
Libra
Scorpio
Capricorn
Aquarius
Pisces

SALLY KIRKMAN

Sagittarius

The Art of Living Well and Finding
Happiness According to Your Star Sign

HODDER

First published in Great Britain in 2018 by Hodder & Stoughton
An Hachette UK company

5

Copyright © Sally Kirkman 2018

The right of Sally Kirkman to be identified as the Author of the
Work has been asserted by her in accordance with the Copyright,
Designs and Patents Act 1988.

All images © Shutterstock.com

A CIP catalogue record for this title is available from the British Library

Hardback ISBN 978 1 473 67686 2

Typeset in Celeste 11.5/17 pt by Palimpsest Book Production Limited,
Falkirk, Stirlingshire

Printed and bound in Great Britain by Clays Ltd, Elcograf S.p.A.

Hodder & Stoughton policy is to use papers that are natural,
renewable and recyclable products and made from wood grown in
sustainable forests. The logging and manufacturing processes are expected
to conform to the environmental regulations of the country of origin.

Hodder & Stoughton Ltd
Carmelite House
50 Victoria Embankment
London EC4Y 0DZ

www.hodder.co.uk

Contents

· · · · · ·

Introduction

• • • • •

Before computers, books or a shared language, people were fascinated by the movement of the stars and planets. They created stories and myths around them. We know that the Babylonians were one of the first people to record the zodiac, a few hundred years BC.

In ancient times, people experienced a close connection to the earth and the celestial realm. The adage 'As above, so below', that the movement of the planets and stars mirrored life on earth and human affairs, made perfect sense. Essentially, we were all one, and ancient people sought symbolic meaning in everything around them.

We are living in a very different world now, in

which scientific truth is paramount; yet many people are still seeking meaning. In a world where you have an abundance of choice, dominated by the social media culture that allows complete visibility into other people's lives, it can be hard to feel you belong or find purpose or think that the choices you are making are the right ones.

It's this calling for something more, the sense that there's a more profound truth beyond the objective and scientific, that leads people to astrology and similar disciplines that embrace a universal truth, an intuitive knowingness. Today astrology has a lot in common with spirituality, meditation, the Law of Attraction, a desire to know the cosmic order of things.

Astrology means 'language of the stars' and people today are rediscovering the usefulness of ancient wisdom. The universe is always talking to you; there are signs if you listen and the more you tune in, the more you feel guided by life. This is one of astrology's significant benefits, helping you to make sense of an increasingly unpredictable world.

Used well, astrology can guide you in making the best possible decisions in your life. It's an essential skill in your personal toolbox that enables you to navigate the ups and downs of life consciously and efficiently.

About this book

Astrology is an ancient art that helps you find meaning in the world. The majority of people to this day know their star sign, and horoscopes are growing increasingly popular in the media and online.

The modern reader understands that star signs are a helpful reference point in life. They not only offer valuable self-insight and guidance, but are indispensable when it comes to understanding other people, and living and working together in harmony.

This new and innovative pocket guide updates the ancient tradition of astrology to make it relevant and topical for today. It distils the wisdom of the star signs into an up-to-date format that's easy to read and digest, and fun and informative too. Covering a broad range of topics, it offers you insight and understanding into many different areas of your life. There are some unique sections you won't find anywhere else.

The style of the guide is geared towards you being able to maximise your strengths, so you can live well and use your knowledge of your star sign to your advantage. The more in tune you are with your zodiac sign, the higher your potential to lead a happy and fulfilled life.

The guide starts with a quick introduction to your star sign, in bullet point format. This not only reveals your star sign's ancient ruling principles, but brings astrology up-to-date, with your star sign mission, an appropriate quote for your sign and how best to describe your star sign in a tweet.

The first chapter is called 'Be True To Your Sign' and is one of the most important sections in the guide. It's a comprehensive look at all aspects of your star sign, helping define what makes you special, and explaining how the rich symbolism of your zodiac sign can reveal more about your character. For example, being born at a specific time of year and in a particular season is significant in itself.

This chapter focuses in depth on the individual attributes of your star sign in a way that's positive and uplifting. It offers a holistic view of your sign and is meant to inspire you. Within this section, you find out the reasons why your star sign traits and characteristics are unique to you.

There's a separate chapter towards the end of the guide that takes this star sign information to a new level. It's called 'Your Cosmic Gifts and Talents' and tells you what's individual about you from your star sign perspective. Most importantly, it highlights your skills and strengths, offering you clear examples of how to make the most of your natural birthright.

The guide touches on another important aspect of your star sign, in the chapters entitled 'Your Shadow Side' and 'Your Star Sign Secrets'. This reveals the potential weaknesses inherent within your star sign, and the tricks and habits you can fall into if you're not aware of them. The star sign secrets might surprise you.

There's guidance here about what you can focus on to minimise the shadow side of your star sign, and this is linked in particular to your opposite sign of the zodiac. You learn how opposing forces complement each other when you hold both ends of the spectrum, enabling them to work together.

Essentially, the art of astrology is about how to find balance in your life, to gain a sense of universal or cosmic order, so you feel in flow rather than pulled in different directions.

Other chapters in the guide provide revealing information about your love life and sex life. There are cosmic tips on how to work to your star sign strengths so you can attract and keep a fulfilling relationship, and lead a joyful sex life. There's also a guide to your love compatibility with all twelve star signs.

Career, money and prosperity is another essential section in the guide. These chapters offer you vital information on your purpose in life, and how to make the most of your potential out in the world. Your star sign skills and strengths are revealed, including what sort of job or profession suits you.

There are also helpful suggestions about what to avoid and what's not a good choice for you. There's a list of traditional careers associated with your star sign, to give you ideas about where you can excel in life if you require guidance on your future direction.

Also, there are chapters in the book on practical matters, like your health and well-being, your food and diet. These recommend the right kind of exercise for you, and how you can increase your vitality and nurture your mind, body and soul, depending on your star sign. There are individual yoga poses and tarot cards that have been carefully selected for you.

Further chapters reveal unique star sign information about your image and style. This includes whether there's a particular fashion that suits you, and how you can accentuate your look and make the most of your body.

There are even chapters that can help you decide where to go on holiday and who with, and how to decorate your home. There are some fun sections, including ideal gifts for your star sign, and ideas for films, books and music specific to your star sign.

Also, the guide has a comprehensive birthday section so you can find out which famous people share your birthday. You can discover who else is born under your star sign, people who may be your role models and whose careers or gifts you can aspire to. There are celebrity examples throughout the guide too, revealing more about the unique characteristics of your star sign.

At the end of the guide, there's a Question and Answer section, which explains the astrological terms used in the guide. It also offers answers to some general questions that often arise around astrology.

This theme is continued in a useful section entitled Additional Information. This describes the symmetry of astrology and shows you how different patterns connect the twelve star signs. If you're a beginner to astrology, this is your next stage, learning about the elements, the modes and the houses.

View this book as your blueprint, your guide to you and your future destiny. Enjoy discovering astrological revelations about you, and use this pocket guide to learn how to live well and find happiness according to your star sign.

A QUICK GUIDE TO SAGITTARIUS

• • • • •

Sagittarius Birthdays: 23 November to 21 December

Zodiac Symbol: The Archer

Ruling Planet: Jupiter

Mode/Element: Mutable Fire

Colour: Purple

Part of the Body: Buttocks, hips and thighs

Day of the Week: Thursday

Top Traits: Enthusiastic, Free-spirited, Visionary

Your Star Sign Mission: to bring joy and laughter into life, to be a reminder that faith and hope are the springboard to abundance and endless possibility

Best At: looking on the bright side, laughing loud, partying, embracing life to the full, starting a journey, playing big, learning and educating self and others, grand gestures, being philosophical

Weaknesses: self-indulgent, excessive, overconfident and unrealistic, clumsy, tactless, blunt

Key Phrase: I explore

Sagittarius Quote: 'If you can dream it, you can do it.' Walt Disney

How to describe Sagittarius in a Tweet: Freedom rules. Fly high, envision & see the world. Lover of justice & truth. Bounces through life like Tigger, clumsy but likeable

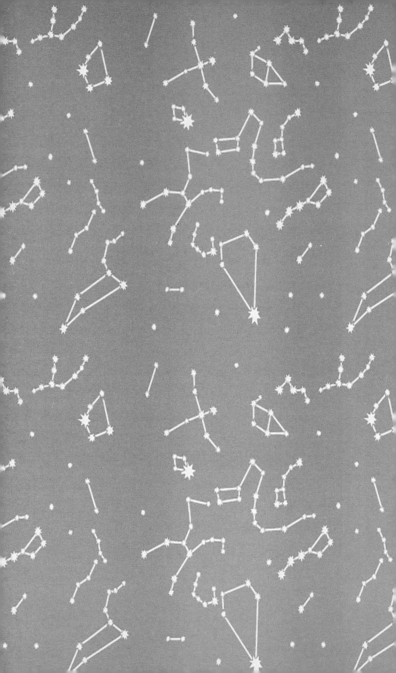

Be True To Your Sign

• • • • •

You are the zodiac's explorer whose outlook on life is optimistic and visionary, and you're always looking for the next adventure. Your gaze is set firmly to the future, ever hopeful of new opportunities and possibilities to come your way. You're a larger than-life character whose immediate response to an invitation is 'Yes'.

Your ruling planet is Jupiter, who was king of the gods in mythology. The word jovial comes from Jove, another of Jupiter's names, and this bestows upon you a cheerful nature. You always look on the bright side of life and you're a joy to be around.

The Sagittarius birthday season comes towards the end of the year when the festive parties are in full swing, and there's a chance to enjoy an excessive few weeks in the run-up to Christmas. If you're a typical Sagittarius, you love the social whirl, as you're a hedonist at heart. A people person to the max, you're often at your happiest when laughter and wine are flowing in equal measure.

You have a great sense of humour, you love to joke and fool about and you like to have fun and make people happy. This is another crucial aspect of your ruling planet, which is associated with a giving and benevolent nature.

Jupiter is the biggest planet in the universe, and everything about your sign of Sagittarius is big, including over-the-top and extravagant gestures and your big-hearted personality. Add to this the fact that you're one of the motivated fire signs, renowned for being spontaneous and enthusiastic, and there's no wonder that you make an immediate and lively impression on other people.

In astrology, your ruler Jupiter could be described as the best planet, because it symbolises opportunity, good fortune, expansiveness and luck. There's a boundless quality to Jupiter that enables you, as a Sagittarius, to believe that you can do anything, and that there's no limit to what's possible.

Jupiter was one of the sky gods, and every Sagittarius believes that the sky is the limit. In fact you probably want to keep going even further, exploring far and wide, pushing back the boundaries.

When you're in full flight, nothing can stop you. Fear won't hold you back, you break through restriction or limitation and you see the positive in even the most demanding or challenging situation. You are an unstoppable force, and this can take you far in life.

You are not, however, one of the most ambitious signs of the zodiac, at least in the way the majority of the world defines ambition. You have big goals in life, but those goals are usually fun and adventurous and meaningful to you personally.

Also, it's rarely about the destination for you, but the journey. Even if you reach a high-profile position or make a significant achievement, your energetic and enthusiastic nature ensures that you keep looking and planning for what's next.

This is the legacy of your zodiac symbol, the Archer, who fires his arrows high into the sky to see where they land. The Archer is brave and bold, future-oriented, and those arrows keep coming. If you're a classic Sagittarius, you are rarely short of ideas or inspiration, and you have a visionary nature. Add to this the fact that you're fearless and willing to take risks, and you can line up some audacious goals in your lifetime.

You are always looking ahead, and you are brilliant at seeing the bigger picture and dreaming up new plans. There's a restless quality to your sign too, a sense of wanderlust, the need to keep moving. You often have a strong desire to see and experience as much as possible in life, and you actively want to learn, gain knowledge and find things out.

This is also connected to the fact that Sagittarius rules the ninth house in the astrology wheel. This is the house of exploration; it's about expanding your world by any means possible, whether physically, mentally, spiritually or in the search for meaning or a higher purpose.

The ninth house rules long-distance travel and is linked to higher education and the quest for knowledge. It's the house of religion and beliefs, truth and justice. This is where your ruler Jupiter resides in his role as divine authority, giver of sound advice, wise and tolerant god.

Without a grand plan or a bigger picture in life, you can roam endlessly or give in to your inner hedonist. When you find your passion, however, the thing in life that fascinates and interests you above all else, you're a person on a mission. You're at your best when you have something to believe in, a purpose. Then you can pursue your personal goals and aims wholeheartedly.

Like all of the fire signs, there's an innocence to the way you approach life, with your sense of childlike wonder and your impulsiveness that wants to play and have fun. You have faith that everything will work out in the end, whether this is backed up by facts or not. You continue to trust implicitly in life, and invariably you follow where life leads.

This does mean that your experience of life is akin to a roller-coaster ride rather than a steady train journey on an even level. This is secretly how you prefer it, as you'd rather live a life full of ups and downs packed with joyful and life-enhancing experiences than get to the end of your days and feel that you've never lived.

You understand inherently that there's a rich seam that runs through your existence in this world, a deep and meaningful learning experience just waiting to be excavated and explored thoroughly. Whatever life throws your way, you say Yes to it. As a Sagittarius, you consider the bigger picture and take a philosophical approach to life, always actively seeking the truth in any given situation.

Your Shadow Side

You are one of the mutable signs of the zodiac, which lends you a dual nature. This is shown clearly in your zodiac symbol, the Archer, who's a centaur, a mythical being that was half man, half horse. The human half of the centaur represents civility and wisdom, whereas the animal half symbolises the centaur's bestial nature, wild and unruly.

You might recognise this split in your character. There's a side to every Sagittarius that's on a mission of truth-seeking or finding the higher purpose and meaning in life. This is when you hold true to noble values, such as honour, faith, justice and social responsibility.

There is, however, a shadow side to your Sagittarius nature that wants to go wild, let rip, live large, and give in to indulgence entirely. This Sagittarius lives an excessive lifestyle, goes way over the top in all areas and can cause complete havoc.

This plays out in different ways. Sometimes it means you throw caution to the winds and romp through life, chasing after adventures and taking wildly extravagant risks with no forethought, care or attention. This can be detrimental to your health, and dangerous too if you don't ensure your safety. The shadow side of your behaviour often impacts detrimentally on your close relationships, if other people get caught up in the Sagittarius whirlwind.

There is another level here, which stems from the fact that you're a fire sign, energetic and spontaneous, and that your ruler Jupiter expands whatever it touches. This makes for a big personality, which can be too much for some people, and downright exhausting.

If you're leaping around like a whirling dervish, wanting to make things happen now, and sort out other people's lives immediately, it can be off-putting. In all the bluster and exuberance, there's no room to check how another person's feeling or even give them a chance to speak.

What can happen is that your ego becomes over-inflated, and you end up avidly pursuing your interests, regardless of anyone else. It's as if you take on the persona of Jupiter – you throw down your thunderbolt and proclaim you're the divine authority.

This is where you can learn from your opposite sign of Gemini, as opposing pairs of the zodiac complement each other. Gemini understands finer detail and focuses on the facts. If you've lost yourself in the excitement and grandiosity of what you're pursuing, a nod to your opposite sign can help you think things through logically and work out a plan. Gemini also acts as a gentle reminder that successful communication is two-way.

Your desire for truth is noble, and you can see through the hype and know if someone's sincere or not. Your impulse to speak out whatever the consequences, however, gets you into trouble. You're not known for your tact and, in fact, you can be downright blunt in your pursuit of honesty.

You know when your shadow side has taken hold when you become boastful in your demeanour, dogmatic in your views or rude in your behaviour. It's your way, or not at all. This is when it's time to rein in your shadow side.

Your Star Sign Secrets

Shhh, don't tell anyone but your greatest fear is that you don't know what you're doing or where you're heading, even though you fool yourself and other people into thinking that everything's going to turn out all right. If you are continually saying out loud: 'It will all work out in the end' or 'I'm handing it all up to God', you might need to admit to yourself and others that you haven't got a clue. It's fine not to know, but it's also helpful to stop and ask for advice or guidance. Once you admit you're feeling lost, or you've made a mistake or taken a wrong turn, then you can get back on track. This is Sagittarius' star sign secret.

You have another secret too, which is that you want everything to happen in an instant. You don't have the patience for taking the slow train to success and happiness; instead, you crave the buzz of the make-or-break deal, a chance to turn your life around overnight. It takes luck, vision, immense self-belief and a fearless nature to live life on the edge. Fortunately, all these traits are available to you as a Sagittarius, and if anyone is going to receive luck at the eleventh hour, it's you.

Your Love Life

Knowing about your star sign is an absolute essential when it comes to love and relationships. Once you understand what drives you, nurtures you and keeps you happy in love, then you can be true to who you are rather than try to be someone you're not.

Plus, once you recognise your weak points when it comes to relationships (and everyone has them), you can learn to moderate them and focus instead on boosting your strengths to find happiness in love.

> **KEY CONCEPTS:** freedom and love, a relationship contract, friends with benefits, sexy adventures, power parting

Cosmic Tip: A relationship that doesn't restrict your freedom suits you best. If you want marriage and commitment, you have to redefine what freedom means to you.

When it comes to love and relationships, it is important to remember that your Sagittarius archetype is the explorer, and it's rare to find a Sagittarius who meets their childhood sweetheart and settles down happily ever after.

That's not to say this is impossible, but you are a free spirit. If you're a typical Sagittarius, you are at your best when you're able to roam far and wide, travel the world and experience as much of life as possible. Therefore, don't rush into marriage and commitment if you sense that a few years down the line you'll be champing at the bit and ready to break free.

Your extrovert and confident personality mean that you find it easy getting to know people. In fact, this can be one of your biggest passions in life, so you usually have a full social circle and plenty of opportunities to meet someone new.

It does take someone unique, however, to catch your attention. You have a penchant for the exotic, and your love of all things foreign means that you often end up with a lover or partner from a different culture or background to your own. As you're the traveller of the zodiac, it makes sense for you to be with a partner from a different country.

Until you're ready to settle down, you may have different lovers around the world, i.e. a man or woman in every port. Or you may have one or more people in your friendship group who you get together with now and again for sex and a good time. Friends with benefits suits Sagittarius' easy-going mentality.

More often than not, you'll be direct and honest about what you want from a lover, partner or relationship. Your ability to be frank and open can be disarming for some people as you don't tend to be diplomatic. Instead, you make it clear up front what your intentions are.

This can come across as uncaring, but actually, it's the reverse. You don't want to lead someone astray, and you would rather be truthful about what you want, even if this comes across like a love contract. You can be hard to pin down emotionally because you veer away from messy entanglements, and playing emotional games is not your style.

That's not to say you won't go all out to win over someone whom you're attracted to, even if they're unavailable. For you, all's fair in love and war, and you have no qualms about trying to win someone's affections. If you believe you're right for each other, you'll give it a good shot.

The thrill of an affair is a strong temptation for you because, as a Sagittarius, an affair adds spice to life; it's a bit dangerous and, very often, a brilliant adventure.

When you do fall in love, it tends to be hook, line and sinker, and experiencing the depths of your emotions can be overwhelming for you. You may become lovesick or lose weight because you're not eating and, at first anyway, you want to be with the object of your desire twenty-four seven. This is where the full extent of your Sagittarius passion is unleashed.

It does, however, take someone special in your life for you to commit to marriage or a long-term relationship. You need a partner who allows you your freedom and won't restrict you; freedom and space are an essential part of a healthy relationship for you. You are rarely someone who's possessive or jealous either, especially once the first flush of love has settled.

If you meet a fellow free spirit, then the two of you can be happy travelling the world together and having big adventures. However, you often benefit from being with a partner who acts as an anchor in your life. Someone you trust implicitly who is there for you day in, day out, and who encourages you to be all you can be. They must be your best friend too, someone who you enjoy spending time with.

Honesty and integrity matter to you in love as in life. You can't bear people who tell lies, and if your partner cheats on you and deceives you, it's hard for you to forgive and forget. Your impulsive nature means that you too can potentially leap into an affair, but ideally you would rather be upfront and direct and explain the reasons why you feel restless. An honest, open confrontation means more to you than lies and deceit, which could end your relationship.

If you choose to go your separate ways, there's a strong possibility that you can do so honestly and openly. A power parting, for example, that's fair and acknowledges what you've meant to each other over the years.

There's a beautiful example of this between two Sagittarius artists, Marina Abramović (30 November) and Ulay (30 November). In 1988, they wanted to embark on a journey that would symbolically define the end of their relationship, so they chose to walk the Great Wall of China from different ends.

Each of them walked 2,500 kilometres, and they met in the middle to hug and say goodbye. What a fabulously fitting and honourable way for two Sagittarius individuals, the travellers of the zodiac, to call time on their relationship.

Your Love Matches

Some star signs are a better love match for you than others. The classic combinations are the other two star signs from the same element as your sign, fire; in Sagittarius' case, Aries and Leo.

You're guaranteed fun and a good laugh with your fellow fire signs, but sometimes you need an extra dimension, something special for you to feel the pull towards settling down. Fun and friendship are important when it comes to a love relationship, but it's a person's spirit that calls to you the most.

It's also important to recognise that any star sign match can be a good match if you're willing to learn from each other and use astrological insight to understand more about what makes the other person tick. Here's a quick guide to your love matches with all twelve star signs:

Sagittarius–Aries: In Your Element

You share a daredevil sense of adventure. Life's for living full on and at top speed, and this can be a courageous and bold relationship with both of you wanting to seek out the next adrenalin rush. Once the spark of passion's brightly lit, there's no stopping you.

Sagittarius–Taurus: Soulmates

Sagittarius and Taurus is at first glance an unlikely pairing. You're the explorer of the zodiac, while

Taurus appreciates routine and home comforts. However, you are both hedonists at heart and share a love of laughter and good times.

Sagittarius–Gemini: Opposites Attract

You are a seeker of truth and deeper meaning in life, while Gemini is continuously on the move, flighty, witty and loves gossip. Together you two can have lots of fun, inspire one another, teach and learn from each other. A youthful couple with a mutual love of life.

Sagittarius–Cancer: Soulmates

Sagittarius and Cancer are poles apart. You are the traveller of the zodiac and Cancer rules home and family. One craves security (Cancer), while the other fights against it (Sagittarius). Finding a home environment that works for you both is the key to happiness.

Sagittarius–Leo: In Your Element

This is a loud and lively pairing as you share a mutual love of parties and living life to the full. Taste-wise there are differences, as you're a back-packer while Leo wants to travel in style. As long as you live the good life together and not apart, this match can not only survive but thrive.

Sagittarius–Virgo: Squaring Up To Each Other

Sagittarius loves everything big and expansive, while Virgo is the god of small things. Virgo must allow you full rein to roam free, and you must pay attention to Virgo's everyday wants and needs. Get the balance right, and you two can be bigger and better together.

Sagittarius–Libra: Sexy Sextiles

You are a free spirit, while Libra needs a partner close by their side. You share a love of the good things in life, and as long as your relationship is full of stimulating experiences, love can thrive. Sharing an interest in an activity or hobby keeps you two interested in each other.

Sagittarius–Scorpio: Next-Door Neighbours

You both thrive on adventure, so there's no shortage of passion between the two of you. Scorpio wants love to be intense and seeks a psychic connection, whereas your freedom-loving sign wants love to be fun. Commitment can be an issue.

Sagittarius–Sagittarius: Two Peas In A Pod

An optimistic and sunny pair, this match loves life and thrives on adventure and new experiences. Laughter is the relationship's lifeblood and keeps your bond warm and vibrant. Freedom has to be a high priority, but as long as you give each other space to roam, this relationship can be a joy.

Sagittarius–Capricorn: Next-Door Neighbours

An unlikely combination at first glance; it's not easy to imagine your larger-than-life sign of Sagittarius and sensible Capricorn as bedmates. However, you are both worldly-wise and if you find a shared ambition, you can work well together and show off your entrepreneurial flair.

Sagittarius–Aquarius: Sexy Sextiles

You and Aquarius are the freedom-lovers of the zodiac, and both want to live life to the full. Commitment is the C-word that neither sign is comfortable with, so there needs to be a broader purpose to stay together for ever. An open relationship suits your combination best.

Sagittarius–Pisces: Squaring Up To Each Other

Sagittarius and Pisces are both ruled by the biggest and most boundless planet in the universe,

Jupiter. You two can encourage each other to try out new things and experience life to the max. With a mutual understanding, you can inspire and enrich each other's lives.

Your Sex Life

· · · · ·

If your ruling planet is anything to go by, you are one of the most promiscuous of lovers. In mythology, Jupiter was a philanderer, and he was continually changing his guise to seduce a new lover.

In reality, you are more likely to be the type of lover who won't commit until you're ready. If two grown adults are attracted to one another and up for sex, that's a fair transaction as far as you're concerned. You don't always associate sex with love, and your free-spirited nature is happy with a physical relationship, no strings attached.

This can be why you might gain something of a reputation for having many lovers before you settle down. If a loving relationship fits into your lifestyle and your current set of life goals, great. If not, you will play the field for as long as you choose.

Sex, like all things in Sagittarius' playground, is best when it's fun. In fact, you're most likely to be swept off your feet and into a lover's bed if they make you laugh. Laughter is a huge aphrodisiac for you, and if you can have a laugh and a joke before, during and after sex, that's a bonus.

In fact, you won't want to hang around for long if your lover turns serious on you or gets too cosy and lovey-dovey. This can be a huge turn off for you if you're not in love and only want the physical experience and a good time.

You see sex as an integral part of your life adventure. You can be up for wild sex or sex that adds a glimmer of danger to your life. You like living on the edge, and you love the thrill of instant attraction, and taking it as far as you both choose.

If you're travelling, you are more than happy to be impulsive and go off with a lover for the night. An illicit encounter where you don't have to swap numbers or names appeals to your thrill-seeking nature.

If someone wants to have sex with you outdoors on the beach or halfway up a mountain, this is the best thing in your book, as you get a kick out of making love in the open. If you come up with a great idea for where to have sex, you'll be more than happy to persuade your lover – or proposition someone new if you're single.

In a loving relationship, it's essential that you keep the spark of love alive by renewing your sexual desires and doing things differently. You love games, so strip poker is an ideal option, or making love in the garden or somewhere there's the possibility you could get caught.

You are a physical lover, especially when you're in good shape, and you're more than willing to try different sex positions. Your inner thighs, buttocks and hips are your number one erogenous zone, so ensure they receive lots of stimulation for ultimate pleasure. As long as sex remains fun and an adventure, you can happily keep going all night.

SAGITTARIUS ON A FIRST DATE

- you make a grand entrance

- laughter and drink must be involved

- if you're bored, you make an excuse and leave

- you bump into someone you know

- you'll be frank about whether sex is on the menu

Your Friends and Family

As a Sagittarius, you make the best friend because you're encouraging and positive, and you're always up for a good time. Admittedly, you prefer friends who are fun rather than dull, and who don't have too many airs and graces, or prudish qualities.

In general, you enjoy being around friends who are as easy-going and fun-loving as you are. Your Sagittarius nose will invariably sniff out the best places where people gather and there's laughter, music and drink flowing.

You're at your happiest around other people and in a buzzing and lively environment. You're invariably one of the last people to leave a party, and you will stay up all night if you're in good company.

Every Sagittarius has a few friends in their inner circle who are much loved and with whom you share everything. This is where your generosity knows no bounds, and you can go to incredible lengths for friends who are dear to your heart. Your kindness is genuinely selfless, and you expect nothing in return for your kind gifts or gestures.

Also, you're fantastic at encouraging your friends to be the best they can be. Even if they're not ready to take risks, you will talk them into being bold and adventurous. You will always be there for your friends no matter what.

If you're a typical Sagittarius, you have different levels of friendship. There are those friends you know inside out, who you love philosophising with and talking about life in depth. At your best, you're an armchair psychologist and give great advice. You're not afraid to speak your mind, you're always straight and direct and you have an opinion about everything.

There's another level of friendship, the people you want to hang out with but nothing more. These are your party mates, good for gossip, fun and get-togethers.

Finally, you have friends in your life who can be influential, and vice versa, and you know how to work your social connections. One of the most famous books on friendship was written by a Sagittarius, Dale Carnegie (24 November) back in 1936. It's called *How To Win Friends and Influence People* and continues to be a bestseller to this day.

As a friend, you're not always 100% reliable, and this is sometimes because you take on too much in your life or you become overly busy. This means you can't keep tabs on everyone, and invariably some friends get dropped.

You are also renowned for being an expert at getting things your way, and this doesn't sit easily with everyone. If you're too demanding or you continually turn up announced and ask too much of your friendships, this can be an issue.

You don't keep secrets well either, and friends often learn this the hard way. It's not that you want to break a confidence, but instead, you want to try to help and sort things out. This is where your lack of tact can cause problems when you forget what's truly important to the other person.

If an issue flares up between you and a friend, you'll confront it head-on. Once it's dealt with openly and honestly, you're prepared to move on, and you're not usually someone who holds a grudge. You know that without your friends, life would be a lot duller and more lonely.

Your loyal nature extends to your wider family as long as no one tries to hold you back or stops you living the life you choose. You want and need freedom of movement from an early age, and it doesn't take the Sagittarius child long before you're ready to spread your wings and leave home.

Some of you run from responsibility, and this can be an issue within your family. You might have relatives who are always asking when you're going to settle down. You don't have time, either, for family who are overly pious or expect you to live by their rules or adopt their moral code. 'Live and let live' is Sagittarius' motto and that applies to all close relationships.

When it comes to parenting and spending time with kids, you're loads of fun, whether you're entertaining friends' children or having adventures with your own. Discipline doesn't come naturally to you, however, and you often encourage kids to run free in life and have the best time.

That being said, there is a side to your Sagittarius nature that can be controlling when you want. This relates to your ruler Jupiter being a divine authority; you often expect other people to live by your code, your truth. In this respect, you can be a strict parent.

You won't usually sacrifice your own life or your freedom for your kids or your partner. Instead, you'll continue to pursue your big personal goals and often, it's the Sagittarius parent with your larger-than-life character who is the one ruling the roost.

Your Health and Well-Being

> **KEY CONCEPTS:** the great outdoors, strong legs and thighs, good times and good food, indulgent lifestyle

A healthy lifestyle is rarely top of the list when it comes to Sagittarius' priorities in life. Being ruled by Jupiter, the planet most linked to hedonism and good times, you would much prefer to have fun than worry about being sensible when it comes to exercise and diet.

Running and jogging are excellent activities for you, especially as Sagittarius rules the hips and thighs. Keeping active is important, but anything that smacks of routine or that you have to do repetitively can be hugely dull in your eyes.

Therefore, you need a good incentive if you're to take on a regular sport or exercise regime. The typical Sagittarius physique is naturally muscular and athletic, so some of you do end up as sports-people; so there's your reason to keep fit.

At other times in your life, you might be keen to lose weight. Jupiter is the planet of expansion and extravagance after all, and a typical indulgent Sagittarius lifestyle means you can quickly put on the pounds.

If you start going to the gym and exercise classes, more likely than not you'll do it excessively, and when you're in the swing of things will probably go at least once a day, if not more. In all areas of life, the classic Sagittarius approach is full on.

The ideal scenario for you is to lead an outdoor lifestyle. You often enjoy walking up hills, going on a trek or learning a sport such as skiing, wind-surfing or climbing, which keeps your body fit and active. You do have to take care, however, because your sign is notoriously clumsy and acci-dent-prone.

The great outdoors though is where you feel most at home, and if you're among a convivial group of people, this is the most pleasurable way for you to stay fit and healthy.

If you're a typical Sagittarius, you hate to feel constrained and you're not someone who takes kindly to being told what to do or having too many rules to abide by. This is another reason why exercise classes can feel like torture, and why you prefer to choose what you want to do and be free to do it as and when.

More than any other sign, you tend to go off the rails, because that's the way you live. Self-discipline and self-control don't come naturally to you, and you often have to work hard to stay on track with any significant goal. This is where that all-important incentive comes in. If you have a strong purpose for what you want to do or a vision of where you want to be, then you can make great strides and be successful.

You are easily influenced by other people and good times. If it's a choice between a big party with friends, staying up all night and having one drink too many, or going to bed early because you want to get up and go for a run, the archetypal Sagittarius will always choose the fun option.

As with all the fire signs, it's beneficial for you to find an activity that acts as a soothing influence upon you; any activity that calms down your abundance of energy, e.g. yoga or meditation. It's also a good idea to focus on positive thinking, which is different to buoyant optimism, something that comes to you naturally.

Being a free spirit, however, is the ultimate Sagittarius feel-good activity. You can't go far wrong bareback riding along a beach as the sun sets with the wind in your hair. This kind of adventure does more for your well-being than any form of hard exercise.

Sagittarius and Food

You are the 'bon viveur' of the zodiac, and your indulgent nature means you love good food, having a drink with friends and enjoying life to the max. When you have big planet Jupiter as your zodiac guardian, there will be times in your life when you also have an expanding waistline, especially if the partying is excessive.

You love food, and you love people. Put the two together and you are the most convivial, warm and generous host. You're often a good cook, not that you tend to follow recipes; instead, you cook intuitively and it usually tastes delicious.

You will always ensure there's more than enough food for everyone, and you expect your guests to have second helpings. Those who ask for third helpings get Brownie points.

Rich and creamy food appeals to your Sagittarius nature, and you love to see a plate stacked full. Sagittarius season marks the run-up to Christmas, a time when tables are laden with an abundance of food and buffets tempt the senses with a smor-gasbord of sumptuous delicacies.

Sagittarius rules all purple berries, including grapes, and mulled wine is the ideal drink for you. Cloves, nutmeg and cinnamon are also ruled by your sign.

A typical Sagittarius likes to eat and you often enjoy a diverse range of cuisine. Jupiter, your planet, is linked to all things foreign, so international food and restaurants are great choices for you. If you're abroad, you always opt for the local speciality. Eating outdoors is a favourite activity, and you love picnics, barbecues and campfire food.

Moderation isn't a word you enjoy hearing, let alone want to adhere to, but it is crucial that you learn to rein in your indulgent nature. If you know you can easily slip into wrong ways when it comes to food and drink, put your enquiring Sagittarius mind to good use and improve your diet and healthy eating knowledge.

Sometimes small tweaks to your diet or lifestyle can have a beneficial effect: for example, only drinking wine with a meal or cutting back on caffeine. Attempts at dietary changes won't work at all if you feel deprived. Instead, trick your mind into thinking that you're allowing yourself indulgence, but in a more measured way.

Do You Look Like A Sagittarius?

Ruled by big planet Jupiter, you are rarely small in any sense. You can be exceptionally tall and have super-long legs; or your big personality might shine through despite a lack of stature. In other words, regardless of your physical size, you make your presence known.

You leap through life, and you have been called the 'Tigger' of the zodiac. There's a spirited bounce to your walk, and you stride out with long steps, swinging your arms. If you're a typical Sagittarius, you're athletic, and sometimes you have the bumps and bruises to show for your enthusiastic and physical approach to life.

You are one of the friendliest of people, and your big smile can be utterly charming. You tend to have great teeth, an oval-shaped face with a long nose and lively eyes. It's your hair that's most noticeable, as you usually wear it long and wild, and that applies to the men as well as the women.

Your Style and Image

You are one of the most natural of all the star signs when it comes to style. You have a fresh-faced look, and Sagittarius women look great with no make-up. Jeans are Sagittarius' uniform, and sportswear and active gear suit you too; you can pull off wearing sweatshirts or hoodies, tracksuit bottoms or leggings, and still look fantastic.

In fact, you often have a wardrobe full of clothes that are made for comfort, clothes in which you can move around easily. You rarely choose expensive items or exclusive fashion designs. This is sensible if you're a typical Sagittarius with a rough-and-tumble lifestyle, as it's not worth spending a fortune on clothes if they're going to get ripped or damaged.

That's not to say you don't love clothes; fashion is one way to show off your exuberant personality. Two Sagittarius fashion designers with a love for colour and extrovert fashion are Gianni Versace (2 December) and John Galliano (28 November). Both of their labels are brilliant at mixing different cultures, being unafraid to break the rules and creating a unique style in the name of fashion.

The classic Sagittarius can happily wear a combination of brightly coloured garments that ensures you stand out from the crowd. You might have items of clothing you've picked up on your travels, which don't fit into everyday fashion. Clothes often purvey your fun sense of humour too;

T-shirts with humorous logos or sweatshirts with fun motifs, for example.

Traditionally, your legs are your best assets. Shorts or skirts with a side split look great on Sagittarius women and tight-fitting trousers look great on both sexes.

Sagittarius men often have a badass style, wild and unruly. You only need to think of the line-up of Frank Zappa (21 December), Jimi Hendrix (27 November) and Samuel L. Jackson (21 December) to get a feeling of how far-out your look can be.

Ultimately, you're not bothered about what other people think or whether your outfit is right for a particular occasion. You wear what you want to wear, regardless of the situation, and you do style your way.

Your Home

Your Ideal Sagittarius Home:

A ranch in the American wilderness, where you can spend all day on your horse rounding up your cattle or sheep. Huge vistas and wide open spaces suit your big character and your love of the outdoors.

You are the sign of the zodiac who's most likely to be a global traveller, and it's often true that, wherever you lay your hat, that's your home. If you're a typical Sagittarius, you're easy-going and laid-back, so when it comes to your living space, it needs to suit your way of life rather than be a designer showcase home.

Walking into a Sagittarius' home is all about seeing how real people live, and you're rarely someone who sits still for long doing nothing. Instead, there needs to be plenty going on in your home to keep you entertained and stimulated.

This can include a widescreen TV, lots of books to read, including travel guides and foreign literature, and, most important of all, souvenirs from your travels. The archetypal Sagittarius has a lust for adventure and, if this is true for you, no doubt there'll be a large map of the world or a travel globe prominent in your home.

You are a larger-than-life character in many respects, and if you're typically tall and athletic, you need a home you can move around in. You don't like to be constricted, and small spaces rarely suit you. An open-plan design would be ideal.

Furniture must be functional rather than luxury, and you can be happy lolling around on an old leather sofa or a futon on the floor. Cushions around a low coffee table are a great idea too. You can be clumsy, so you don't want too many delicate items around your home or too much furniture to bump into.

If you're into interior design and you have a big home, you'll go for large statement pieces, like colourful vases to waist-height and dramatic stand-out pieces of furniture. You tend to go over the top with decorating and furnishing, unleashing the extravagant side of your Sagittarius character.

You like bright colours, such as purple, royal blue and pillar-box red. Spanish Moorish homeware with its multicoloured design appeals to you more than anything white or plain. Wall-hangings often have pride of place in your home, and plenty of throws and comfortable accessories too.

You're not usually bothered about everything coordinating or looking impressive. Instead, your home is for living in, socialising and entertaining. Having space where friends can come round, hang out and have fun suits you better than a home that's perfect to look at, but soulless and empty.

If you're an active Sagittarius, you have to take into account where to keep your sports gear, e.g. your muddy boots, your rucksack, your bicycle, your climbing equipment, your gym bag. Having more than one wet room or shower room is also a great idea, and imperative if you don't live alone.

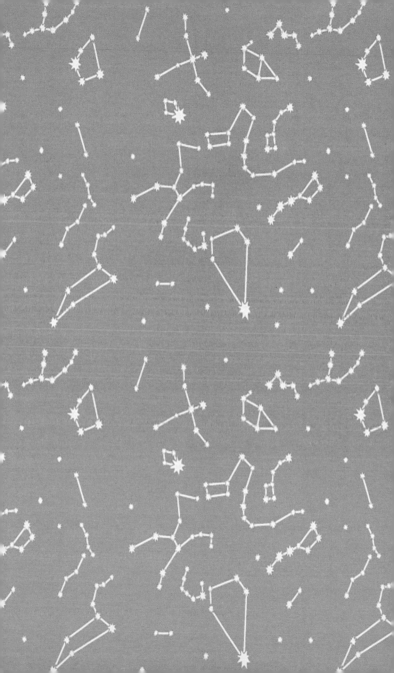

Your Star Sign Destinations

IDEAS FOR SAGITTARIUS:

- *celebrating Carnival in Brazil*

- *an African animal safari*

- *a camper van holiday in Australasia*

Did you know that many cities and countries are ruled by a particular star sign? This is based on when a country was founded, although sometimes, depending on their history, places have more than one star sign attributed to them.

This can help you decide where to go on holiday, and it can also be why there are certain places where you feel at home straight away.

You are the traveller of the zodiac and, if you're a classic Sagittarius, you will want to see as much of the world as possible. You love exploring different countries and cultures and, at least once in your lifetime, it's essential to go on a long back-packing holiday.

Being in different locations inspires you and enables you to think big. In fact, you might be the type of Sagittarius who chooses to work to live rather than live to work and is always saving up money for the next big adventure.

Ideally, you would opt for a long holiday so you can explore a new place to the full. If you're travelling to the other side of the world, it makes sense to give yourself time to deal with your jet lag, visit any relatives or friends and see as much of a country as possible.

You rarely like to sit around doing nothing on holiday; instead, you enjoy activity holidays, where you can get fit and see the sights at the same time. This might include trekking, camping wild, canoeing down a river or going on a pilgrimage.

You often have a bigger purpose behind a trip, whether you're taking on a charity challenge, set yourself a goal of walking a major trail or are seeking a spiritual experience.

You're not averse to a week in the sun with your mates, especially if sun, sea, sex and booze are included, and it is essential to let your hedonistic, party spirit out to play sometimes. You understand inherently, however, that travel has more to offer, and it's often your search for meaning in life that leads you to far-flung places and exotic destinations.

Countries ruled by Sagittarius include Spain, Australia, Hungary, South Africa.

Cities ruled by Sagittarius include Sheffield in the UK; Budapest in Hungary; Stuttgart and Cologne in Germany; Toronto in Canada; Naples in Italy

Your Career and Vocation

Two of your top traits are your dynamic enthusiasm and your bursting-with-life joyful personality. Add to this the fact that you believe anything's possible, and it's no surprise that some Sagittarius individuals start out in their chosen career very young. You were born raring to go and ready to make a noise.

Two child stars who started as 'Mouseketeers' in the Mickey Mouse Club in the States are singers Britney Spears (2 December) and Christina Aguilera (18 December). Vanessa Hudgens (14 December) is another Sagittarius who was making movies in her teens, and the hugely successful Disney High School Musical films established her reputation.

Walt Disney (5 December) himself was a Sagittarius, and the entertainment world is a popular career choice for you. The wonder and magic of Disney embody one side of your irrepressible joyful Sagittarius nature. Some of you never lose that youthful spirit and exuberant confidence, which can open doors of its own accord.

You don't fit easily into the nine-to-five lifestyle, and you might actively choose a career where you can work unusual hours, outside the confines of ordinary life. Casinos and cruise ships both have their appeal for your fun-loving nature. The last thing you want when it comes to a job or profession is to get stuck in a rut, as you quickly grow bored.

In fact, you will often do whatever it takes to stay unfettered and free of responsibility, which can open up some exciting career or life choices for you. You might decide to be a student for life, and find a way to keep being paid to do research, learn and expand your knowledge. You could go from college or university into a teaching role that offers you long holidays, or the chance to take a sabbatical and teach abroad.

Travel and an international lifestyle always appeal to you as a Sagittarius. If you can find a way to fund your love of travel through your career, so much the better. You might choose to work in a travel organisation, primarily if the perks include free trips, or take on an adventure role as a tour guide, visiting destinations off the beaten track.

You could pick a profession that involves a skill or talent that could take you abroad. For example, if you love a sport and you become good enough to represent your country. An alternative plan is that you go on holiday but never come home and, instead, fulfil a dream to work in a bar on the beach or set up a watersports company.

The ideal work scenario for your free-spirited sign is the laptop lifestyle, where you can choose to work from anywhere in the world. This is the territory of the entrepreneur and is an excellent choice for a Sagittarius. To be successful, you need to be willing to take risks and have a big vision and the confidence and enthusiasm to promote or market yourself, your product, your ideas.

This kind of career and lifestyle feeds your freedom-loving spirit and fuels the side of your nature that loves to take a gamble. What you need to be careful of, however, is that you don't take on too much or say Yes to everything. Trust your intuitive fire sign nature to know which opportunities are worth following and which to turn down.

Team up with other people who complement your skills as well, and recognise your strengths and weaknesses. You're not great with details or doing tedious admin-type work.

Also, it is helpful for you to have someone in your life who's a realist and keeps your feet on the ground, especially if you work for yourself. You can spin huge fantasies and let your imagination roam free, but ensure that whatever you become involved in, you have a high chance of turning your dreams into reality.

It's often said about your sign of Sagittarius that you fall into one of two camps: you want either to see the world or save the world. If you fit into the latter category, then pursue a career whereby you can get to the truth or see justice done.

Certain aspects of the law suit your philosophical nature; you might be keen to walk the beat as a police officer or enter into a profession that champions the underdog and backs philanthropic causes. You thrive under pressure as long as you have someone else to organise your busy diary.

Publishing and the media are associated with Sagittarius, as are all forms of global communication. You are often adept at finding the meaning within facts or information. Ultimately, you are drawn towards a career or vocation that's fun, exciting or makes a difference.

If you're seeking inspiration for a new job, take a look at the list below, which reveals the traditional careers that come under the Sagittarius archetype:

TRADITIONAL SAGITTARIUS CAREERS

explorer
adventure tour guide
travel agent

entrepreneur
professional horse rider
long distance runner
athlete
international lawyer
freedom fighter
police officer
publisher
teacher
spiritual leader
vicar
philosopher
publicist
comedian
film director
dream interpreter
visionary coach

Your Money and Prosperity

> **KEY CONCEPTS:** high stakes, win big or lose it all, big-hearted gestures vs. frugal spending, money as freedom, experiences over possessions

You make an excellent entrepreneur, with your big vision and willingness to take risks. This means that when it comes to money, you often prefer a high-stakes approach to life, as there's a side to your Sagittarius nature that loves a gamble.

In fact, you are the complete opposite of the individual who wants to work in a regular job and save diligently for the future. Instead, your approach to money is more likely to be 'double or quits'. If life were a hand of poker, you would always choose to go all in. You'd rather win big or lose everything, and there are times in your life when you will probably act out this scenario.

Also, your Sagittarius nature is extravagant, and you won't think twice about making an impulsive purchase or treating the ones you love. You rarely give a little, either, but are much more likely to give a lot.

If big money does come into your life, it doesn't stay there for ever. You might invest some of it in art or property, business or investments, but you would also be sure to give a good part of it away. What you have, you are more than happy to share around, and the archetypal Sagittarius is a philanthropist.

Money tends to mean different things to you than it does to other people. For starters, if you're a typical Sagittarius, money equals freedom, and you're far more likely to spend what you have on experiences than on possessions. This fits your easy-come, easy-go lifestyle that favours living life to the full rather than saving up for your retirement.

In fact, even though you generally have your eye on the future, you don't always when it comes to money and security. This is because scarcity is a concept that is barely recognised in the Sagittarius lexicon. You are one of only two signs of the zodiac ruled by Jupiter, the planet of bounty and abundance, and, whatever your financial situation, you trust that life will provide for you.

You have endless amounts of optimism and good-will, and a typical Sagittarius believes in karma. You usually make enough good connections in your lifetime that you have people who can repay you for the favours and generosity you've shown them, if and when necessary.

You do meet some Sagittarius individuals who aren't interested in money at all and would rather lead a frugal lifestyle. You might be happy backpacking around the world, for example, and only work to earn enough money to feed yourself, have a roof over your head and keep travelling.

Sometimes, the wealthiest of Sagittarius individuals also have a frugal streak. Take J. Paul Getty (15 December), for example, who was one of the most affluent individuals of his day but was notably frugal. He was famous for negotiating his grandson's kidnapping ransom; he wouldn't pay the first demand but, after he received an ear in the post, he agreed to a second – lower – demand.

He defended his actions by saying it was a matter of principle. If he'd given in immediately, it could have triggered copycat kidnappings and set an unhealthy precedent for other criminals or terrorists.

You could have all the money in the world and you would still choose to spend it or use it in a way that best fits your Sagittarius principles or your love of life. It's rarely about the money itself for you, but instead what it represents and means to you.

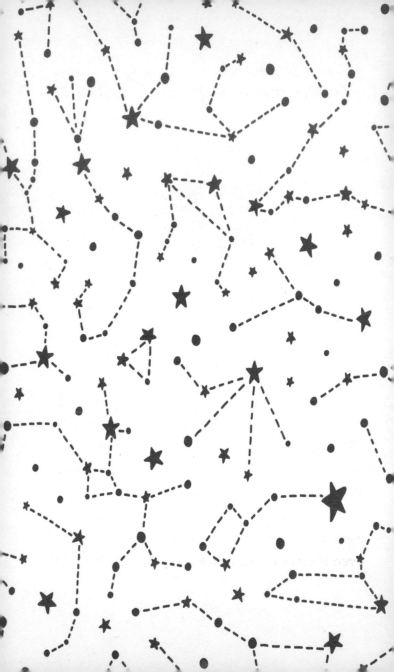

Your Cosmic Gifts and Talents

Explorer

You are the traveller of the zodiac, and your planet Jupiter is associated with foreign connections and all things international. You might become a travel blogger, or go the whole hog and choose to visit all the countries of the world. The archetypal Sagittarius is a nomad, a traveller of life, and your identity is not always defined by your nationality. Even if you can't or won't travel physically, don't rule out the possibility of being a cosmopolitan thinker, an avid reader of international writing or world philosophies. Explore life your way.

Strong Thighs

If you're a typical Sagittarius, you have great thighs and legs. Take legendary singer Tina Turner (26 November), for example, who insured her legs for over $3 million. Or actress and activist Jane Fonda (21 December), who effectively began the exercise video craze with her bestselling DVD, *Jane Fonda's Workout*. As a Sagittarius, you often excel in sports such as horse riding, football and athletics. Whether you climb a mountain, run a marathon or join a dance craze, keep those thighs and legs active and robust.

Make Them Laugh

Every Sagittarius needs a purpose in life, and a purpose to bring joy into the world and make people laugh is more than enough. You are a natural comedian, and many of you end up in the world of comedy where your big and outrageous personality is allowed full rein. Some classic examples are Billy Connolly (24 November), Bette Midler (1 December) and Richard Pryor (1 December). Even if you don't choose to be a comedy star, you can still spread happiness, positive vibes, joy and laughter.

Larger Than Life

If you're a typical Sagittarius, you rarely do anything in a small, unnoticeable way. Instead, you prefer to leap in feet first, go big and be visible. This characteristic of your sign can play out in different ways. For example, you might be a flamboyant Sagittarius like multi-talented Noël Coward (16 December), be tall and noticeable like TV presenter Richard Osman (28 November), who's six feet seven inches, or love galloping like tall comedian Miranda Hart (14 December). Whatever you choose, it's your Sagittarius birthright to flounce through life and get yourself noticed. Be extravagant, be exuberant, be larger than life.

Adopt A Belief System

It suits your Sagittarius profile to find something you believe in and which helps you make sense of the world and your place within it. You often seek a way of thinking that takes you beyond yourself and the personal, and gives you a broader perspective on life. This might be a religion, like Buddhism or Christianity, or a spiritual belief that connects you to nature, the cosmos or the divine. You may change your beliefs throughout your lifetime, but whenever you find a belief that's right for you, you expand your world.

Truth Junkie

Honest to a fault and, at times, blunt and direct, it's hard for you as a Sagittarius not to tell the truth. You say it as it is and you invariably believe that the truth will set you free. It's a similar story when it comes to finding out the truth. You will jump through any number of hoops to get to the truth of the matter, whether you're a hotshot lawyer or you want to find out what the gossip really means. You like people who are genuine and sincere, and you live by strong principles and are true to your own spirit. You're a truth junkie; therefore, be the zodiac's upholder of the truth.

Create An Epic

You're ruled by big planet Jupiter, you're broad-minded and you have a vast range of vision. You are, therefore, destined to do something epic. This shows in the film world, and even though there are famous Sagittarius actors, you're more renowned as the film director; look at big names Steven Spielberg (18 December), Ridley Scott (30 November), Alfonso Cuarón (28 November) and Kathryn Bigelow (27 November).

As the director, you oversee the whole project, you hold everything in your grasp and bring all the diverse elements together – easy for a Sagittarius. This flair for the epic can also be seen in the philosophical and mystical art of William Blake (28 November) and the grandeur of Beethoven's (16 December) symphonies. This is where you excel in life, so create your epic.

Films, Books, Music

• • • • •

Films: *Knocked Up*, director, Judd Apatow (6 December) or *The Hangover*, director, Todd Phillips (20 December) or *The Secret Life Of Walter Mitty*, director/co-producer/star Ben Stiller (30 November), from the book by James Thurber (8 December)

Books: *Gulliver's Travels* by Jonathan Swift (30 November) or the Chronicles of Narnia series by C. S. Lewis (29 November)

Music: 'Purple Haze' by Jimi Hendrix (27 November) or 'Light My Fire' by the Doors, lead singer Jim Morrison (8 December) or any tracks by contemporary megastar Taylor Swift (13 December)

YOGA POSE:

High Lunge: opens the hips, stretches
and tones the thighs

TAROT CARD:

Wheel of Fortune

GIFTS TO BUY A SAGITTARIUS:

- poker set
- purple passport holder
- Snoopy sweatshirt
- active sportswear
- travel cosmetics
- Manolo Blahnik shoes
- adult Tigger costume
- National Geographic Society membership
- a day at the races
- Star Gift – round-the-world airline ticket

Sagittarius Celebrities Born On Your Birthday

NOVEMBER

 (Scarlett Johansson – born on the cusp, see Q&A)

 Zoë Ball, Kelly Brook, Miley Cyrus, Alison Mosshart

 Dale Carnegie, Billy Connolly, Ian Botham, Katherine Heigl

Joe DiMaggio, Imran Khan, Bruno Tonioli, Christina Applegate, Amy Grant

 Charles Schulz, Rich Little, Tina Turner, Natasha Bedingfield, Rita Ora

 Bill Nye, Bruce Lee, Jimi Hendrix, Manolo Blahnik, Michael Vartan, Kathryn Bigelow, Caroline Kennedy

 William Blake, Alfonso Cuarón, Ed Harris, Anna Nicole Smith, John Galliano, Martin Clunes, Jon Stewart, Richard Osman, Randy Newman, Trey Songz

 C. S. Lewis, Jackie Stallone, Diane Ladd, John Mayall, Don Cheadle, Simon Amstell, Anna Faris

 Mark Twain, Winston Churchill, Ridley Scott, Ryan Murphy, Billy Idol, Terrence Malick, Mandy Patinkin, Lorraine Kelly, Chrissy Teigen, Gary Lineker, Ben Stiller,

Elisha Cuthbert, Robert Kirkman, Clay Aiken, Kaley Cuoco, Marina Abramović

DECEMBER

 Woody Allen, Richard Pryor, Bette Midler, Sarah Silverman, Emily Mortimer, Zoë Kravitz,

 Gianni Versace, Lucy Liu, Nelly Furtado, Britney Spears, Monica Seles

 Maria Callas, Ozzy Osbourne, Julianne Moore, Daryl Hannah, Brendan Fraser, Holly Marie Combs, Amanda Seyfried, Jenna Dewan, Andy Grammer

 Rainer Maria Rilke, Jeff Bridges, Pamela Stephenson, Marisa Tomei, Jay-Z, Tyra Banks

5 Walt Disney, Fritz Lang, Little Richard

 6 David Brubeck, Nick Park, Andrew Flintoff, Judd Apatow, Janine Turner

7 Ellen Burstyn, Sue Johnston, Tom Waits, Damien Rice, Nicole Appleton, Aaron Carter, Nicholas Hoult

8 Diego Rivera, Sammy Davis Jr, David Carradine, Jim Morrison, Kim Basinger, Teri Hatcher, Sinćad O'Connor, Dominic Monaghan, Sébastien Chabal, Nicky Minaj, Ian Somerhalder

 9 Kirk Douglas, Judi Dench, John Malkovich, Donny Osmond, Felicity Huffman, Jesse Metcalfe, Kat Bjelland

 10 Clive Anderson, Kenneth Branagh, Susanna Reid, Brian Molko, Raven-Symoné, Teyana Taylor, Tara Subkoff

Christina Onassis, Ben Shephard, Jermaine Jackson, Mo'Nique, Nikki Six, Marco Pierre White

 Edward G. Robinson, Frank Sinatra, Dionne Warwick, Paula Wagner, Robert Lindsay, Bill Nighy, Jasper Conran, Will Carling, Jennifer Connelly, Lucas Hedges, Mayim Bialik

 Dick van Dyke, Christopher Plummer, Jim Davidson, Steve Buscemi, Jamie Foxx, Amy Lee, Sara Cox, James Kyson, Taylor Swift

 Nostradamus, Patty Duke, Spike Jones, Jane Birkin, Vanessa Hudgens, Natascha McElhone, Yotam Ottolenghi, Miranda Hart, Michael Owen

J. Paul Getty, Don Johnson, Frankie Dettori, Adam Brody

16 Jane Austen, Philip K. Dick, Arthur C. Clarke, Noël Coward, Christopher Biggins, Miranda Otto, Benjamin Bratt, Zara Larsson, Theo James, Anna Popplewell

 17 Paula Radcliffe, Milla Jovovich, Stella Tennant

 18 Betty Grable, Celia Johnson, Keith Richards, Steven Spielberg, Jay Bakker, Ray Liotta, Brad Pitt, Robson Green, Katie Holmes, Christina Aguilera, Ashley Benson, Sia

 19 Édith Piaf, Béatrice Dalle, Jennifer Beals, Richard Hammond, Jake Gyllenhaal, Alyssa Milano, Jamie Hince

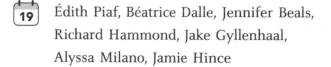 **20** Uri Geller, Jenny Agutter, Billy Bragg, Lara Stone, Jonah Hill, Todd Phillips

21 Phil Donahue, Ray Romano, Jane Fonda, Frank Zappa, Chris Evert, Kiefer

Sutherland, Julie Delpy, Samuel L. Jackson, Emmanuel Macron

 (Robin and Maurice Gibb – born on the cusp, see Q&A)

Q&A Section

• • • • •

Q. What is the difference between a Sun sign and a Star sign?

A. They are the same thing. The Sun spends one month in each of the twelve star signs every year, so if you were born on 1 January, you are a Sun Capricorn. In astronomy, the Sun is termed a star rather than a planet, which is why the two names are interchangeable. The term 'zodiac sign', too, means the same as Sun sign and Star sign and is another way of describing which one of the twelve star signs you are, e.g. Sun Capricorn.

Q. What does it mean if I'm born on the cusp?

A. Being born on the cusp means that you were born on a day when the Sun moves from one of the twelve zodiac signs into the next. However, the Sun doesn't change signs at the same time each year. Sometimes it can be a day earlier or a day later. In the celebrity birthday section of the book, names in brackets mean that this person's birthday falls into this category.

If you know your complete birth data, including the date, time and place you were born, you can find out definitively what Sun sign you are. You do this by either checking an ephemeris (a planetary table) or asking an astrologer. For example, if a baby were born on 20 January 2018, it would be Sun Capricorn if born before 03:09 GMT or Sun Aquarius if born after 03:09 GMT. A year earlier, the Sun left Capricorn a day earlier and entered Aquarius on 19 January 2017, at 21:24 GMT. Each year the time changes are slightly different.

Q. Has my sign of the zodiac changed since I was born?

A. Every now and again, the media talks about a new sign of the zodiac called Ophiuchus and about there now being thirteen signs. This means that you're unlikely to be the same Sun sign as you always thought you were.

This method is based on fixing the Sun's movement to the star constellations in the sky, and is called 'sidereal' astrology. It's used traditionally in India and other Asian countries.

The star constellations are merely namesakes for the twelve zodiac signs. In western astrology, the zodiac is divided into twelve equal parts that are in sync with the seasons. This method is called 'tropical' astrology. The star constellations and the zodiac signs aren't the same.

Astrology is based on a beautiful pattern of symmetry (see Additional Information) and it wouldn't be the same if a thirteenth sign were introduced into the pattern. So never fear, no one is going to have to say their star sign is Ophiuchus, a name nobody even knows how to pronounce!

Q. Is astrology still relevant to me if I was born in the southern hemisphere?

A. Yes, astrology is unquestionably relevant to you. Astrology's origins, however, were founded in the northern hemisphere, which is why the Spring Equinox coincides with the Sun's move into Aries, the first sign of the zodiac. In the southern hemisphere, the seasons are reversed. Babylonian, Egyptian and Greek and Roman astrology are the forebears of modern-day astrology, and all of these civilisations were located in the northern hemisphere.

• • • • •

Q. Should I read my Sun sign, Moon sign and Ascendant sign?

A. If you know your horoscope or you have drawn up an astrology wheel for the time of your birth, you will be aware that you are more than your Sun sign. The Sun is the most important star in the sky, however, because the other planets revolve around it, and your horoscope in the media is based on Sun signs. The Sun represents your essence, who you are striving to become throughout your lifetime.

118

The Sun, Moon and Ascendant together give you a broader impression of yourself as all three reveal further elements about your personality. If you know your Moon and Ascendant signs, you can read all three books to gain further insight into who you are. It's also a good idea to read the Sun sign book that relates to your partner, parents, children, best friends, even your boss for a better understanding of their characters too.

Q. Is astrology a mix of fate and free will?

A. Yes. Astrology is not causal, i.e. the planets don't cause things to happen in your life; instead, the two are interconnected, hence the saying 'As above, so below'. The symbolism of the planets' movements mirrors what's happening on earth and in your personal experience of life.

You can choose to sit back and let your life unfold, or you can decide the best course of action available to you. In this way, you are combining your fate and free will, and this is one of astrology's major purposes in life. A knowledge of astrology can help you live more authentically, and it offers you a fresh perspective on how best to make progress in your life.

Q. What does it mean if I don't identify with my Sun sign? Is there a reason for this?

A. The majority of people identify with their Sun sign, and it is thought that one route to fulfilment is to grow into your Sun sign. You do get the odd exception, however.

For example, a Pisces man was adamant that he wasn't at all romantic, mystical, creative or caring, all typical Pisces archetypes. It turned out he'd spent the whole of his adult life working in the oil industry and lived primarily on the sea. Neptune is one of Pisces' ruling planets and god of the sea and Pisces rules all liquids, including oil. There's the Pisces connection.

Q. What's the difference between astrology and astronomy?

A. Astrology means 'language of the stars', whereas astronomy means 'mapping of the stars'. Traditionally, they were considered one discipline, one form of study and they coexisted together for many hundreds of years. Since the dawn of the Scientific Age, however, they have split apart.

Astronomy is the scientific strand, calculating and logging the movement of the planets, whereas astrology is the interpretation of the movement of the stars. Astrology works on a symbolic and intuitive level to offer guidance and insight. It reunites you with a universal truth, a knowingness that can sometimes get lost in place of an objective, scientific truth. Both are of value.

Q. What is a cosmic marriage in astrology?

A. One of the classic indicators of a relation-ship that's a match made in heaven is the union of the Sun and Moon. When they fall close to each other in the same sign in the birth charts of you and your partner, this is called a cosmic marriage. In astrology, the Sun and Moon are the king and queen of the heavens; the Sun is a masculine energy, and the Moon a feminine energy. They represent the eternal cycle of day and night, yin and yang.

Q. What does the Saturn Return mean?

A. In traditional astrology, Saturn was the furthest planet from the Sun, representing boundaries and the end of the universe. Saturn is linked to karma and time, and represents authority, structure and responsibility. It takes Saturn twenty nine to thirty years to make a complete cycle of the zodiac and return to the place where it was when you were born.

This is what people mean when they talk about their Saturn Return; it's the astrological coming of age. Turning thirty can be a soul-searching time, when you examine how far you've come in life and whether you're on the right track. It's a watershed moment, a reality check and a defining stage of adulthood. The decisions you make during your Saturn Return are crucial, whether they represent endings or new commitments. Either way, it's the start of an important stage in your life path.

Additional Information

• • • • •

The Symmetry of Astrology

There is a beautiful symmetry to the zodiac (see horoscope wheel). There are twelve zodiac signs, which can be divided into two sets of 'introvert' and 'extrovert' signs, four elements (fire, earth, air, water), three modes (cardinal, fixed, mutable) and six pairs of opposite signs.

One of the values of astrology is in bringing opposites together, showing how they complement each other and work together and, in so doing, restore unity. The horoscope wheel represents the cyclical nature of life.

Aries (*March 21–April 19*)
Taurus (*April 20–May 20*)
Gemini (*May 21–June 20*)
Cancer (*June 21–July 22*)
Leo (*July 23–August 22*)
Virgo (*August 23–September 22*)
Libra (*September 23–October 23*)
Scorpio (*October 24–November 22*)
Sagittarius (*November 23–December 21*)
Capricorn (*December 22–January 20*)
Aquarius (*January 21–February 18*)
Pisces (*February 19–March 20*)

ELEMENTS

There are four elements in astrology and three signs allocated to each. The elements are:

fire – Aries, Leo, Sagittarius
earth – Taurus, Virgo, Capricorn
air – Gemini, Libra, Aquarius
water – Cancer, Scorpio, Pisces

What each element represents:

Fire – fire blazes bright and fire types are inspirational, motivational, adventurous and love creativity and play

Earth – earth is grounding and solid, and earth rules money, security, practicality, the physical body and slow living

Air – air is intangible and vast and air rules thinking, ideas, social interaction, debate and questioning

Water – water is deep and healing and water rules feelings, intuition, quietness, relating, giving and sharing

MODES

There are three modes in astrology and four star signs allocated to each. The modes are:

cardinal – Aries, Cancer, Libra, Capricorn
fixed – Taurus, Leo, Scorpio, Aquarius
mutable – Gemini, Virgo, Sagittarius, Pisces

What each mode represents:

Cardinal – The first group represents the leaders of the zodiac, and these signs love to initiate and take action. Some say they're controlling.

Fixed – The middle group holds fast and stands the middle ground and acts as a stable, reliable companion. Some say they're stubborn.

Mutable – The last group is more willing to go with the flow and let life drift. They're more flexible and adaptable and often dual-natured. Some say they're all over the place.

INTROVERT AND EXTROVERT SIGNS/ OPPOSITE SIGNS

The introvert signs are the earth and water signs and the extrovert signs are the fire and air signs. Both sets oppose each other across the zodiac.

The 'introvert' earth and water oppositions are:

- Taurus – • Scorpio
- Cancer – • Capricorn
- Virgo – • Pisces

The 'extrovert' air and fire oppositions are:

- Aries – • Libra
- Gemini – • Sagittarius
- Leo – • Aquarius

THE HOUSES

The houses of the astrology wheel are an additional component to Sun sign horoscopes. The symmetry that is inherent within astrology remains, as the wheel is divided into twelve equal sections, called 'houses'. Each of the twelve houses is governed by one of the twelve zodiac signs.

There is an overlap in meaning as you move round the houses. Once you know the symbolism of all the star signs, it can be fleshed out further by learning about the areas of life represented by the twelve houses.

The houses provide more specific information if you choose to have a detailed birth chart reading.

This is based not only on your day of birth, which reveals your star sign, but also your time and place of birth. Here's the complete list of the meanings of the twelve houses and the zodiac sign they are ruled by:

1 – **Aries:** self, physical body, personal goals

2 – **Taurus:** money, possessions, values

3 – **Gemini:** communication, education, siblings, local neighbourhood

4 – **Cancer:** home, family, roots, the past, ancestry

5 – **Leo:** creativity, romance, entertainment, children, luck

6 – **Virgo:** work, routine, health, service

7 – **Libra:** relationships, the 'other', enemies, contracts

8 – **Scorpio:** joint finances, other peoples' resources, all things hidden and taboo

9 – **Sagittarius:** travel, study, philosophy, legal affairs, publishing, religion

10 – **Capricorn:** career, vocation, status, reputation

11 – **Aquarius:** friends, groups, networks, social responsibilities

12 – **Pisces:** retreat, sacrifice, spirituality

A GUIDE TO LOVE MATCHES

The star signs relate to each other in different ways depending on their essential nature. It can also be helpful to know the pattern they create across the zodiac. Here's a quick guide that relates to the chapter on Love Matches:

Two Peas In A Pod – the same star sign

Opposites Attract – star signs opposite each other

Soulmates – five or seven signs apart, and a traditional 'soulmate' connection

In Your Element – four signs apart, which means you share the same element

Squaring Up To Each Other – three signs apart, which means you share the same mode

Sexy Sextiles – two signs apart, which means you're both 'introverts' or 'extroverts'

Next Door Neighbours – one sign apart, different in nature but often share close connections